Floral Design for Weddings

Wedding Floral Design Course
Study Unit 1
of a Twelve Unit Program

www.InstituteOfWeddings.com

Leader Lifestyle Media
International Institute of Weddings™
The Fundamentals of Wedding Floral Design

This publication has been developed with the intent to provide accurate and authoritative information with regard to the subject matter covered. It is sold with the understanding that the publisher is not engaged in rendering legal, accounting, or other professional advice. If legal advice or other professional assistance is required, the services of a competent attorney, accountant, or other professional consultant should be sought. The publisher and author make no guarantees of performance results or success. Individual success rates will depend on a variety of factors beyond the control of the publisher. Because skill levels and conditions vary, the author and publisher disclaim any liability for unsatisfactory results. Follow the manufacturer's instructions for any tools and supplies used to complete projects in this publication. Exercise caution at all times when working with tools and supplies, and when undertaking any of the projects in this publication. The author and publisher are not responsible for any injury, loss or damage caused by the use of instructions or information in this publication, or by the use of tools and materials. Neither the author or the publisher accepts any responsibility for any liabilities resulting from the actions of any of the parties involved.

Proprietary Information /
Intellectual Property Notice

LEGAL WARNING

PERSONAL USE LICENSE

"A floral decoration should be a celebration of nature, reflecting all its colors, shapes, textures, and spontaneous movement. It is the result of a combination of a few easily learned skills – and imagination in abundance"

~ Kenneth Turner
Internationally Acclaimed Floral Designer

Contents

Foreword

Exclusively Offered by The International Institute of Weddings, the twelve unit Fundamentals of Wedding Floral Design course will qualify you to become a *Certified Wedding Floral Designer™* – a trademarked designation you can only receive through the Institute of Weddings.

This highly specialized Wedding Floral Design course is *the first and only program available anywhere in the world* to offer *distance education focusing exclusively on designing flowers for weddings.* The course has been offered by The International Institute of Weddings since 1999, with thousands of happy students around the world, and is constantly kept up to date. We're excited to welcome you!

Do you have an interest in floral design and a passion for weddings?

The Fundamentals of Wedding Floral Design Course by the International Institute of Weddings is a highly specialized home study course focusing *exclusively* on wedding floral design.

That's correct – *exclusively* wedding floral design. No funeral flowers or hospital arrangements like the lessons in so many other floral design courses – instead, we'll focus intensively on designing *flowers for weddings* – and only weddings.

After all, weddings are where the glamour and excitement is. If your passion is *weddings*, funeral flowers simply won't inspire you, so we've designed a program with laser sharp focus, for people who are interested in *weddings* - people just like *you.*

And if you're thinking of turning your floral design skills into a *business, career*, or even some *extra income in your spare time*, **weddings are DEFINITELY where the money is.** Weddings are *big business*, and they are a whopping $45 billion dollar industry!

Introduction to this course

Welcome to the first unit of the twelve-unit *Fundamentals of Wedding Floral Design Course* by the prestigious *International Institute of Weddings.*

The complete course is divided into 12 individual units to give you a very thorough and fully comprehensive understanding and working knowledge of wedding floral design so that when you have completed all units, you will have mastered the necessary skills to design beautiful flowers for weddings!

Each unit lays the foundation for what you will learn in the units that follow. Think of each unit as an individual floral design class.

The material contained in this training manual is the material for the first unit of the 12 unit course. If you enjoy what you are learning here in Unit 1 and would like to proceed on to the other eleven units of the course, you will have the opportunity to do so by enrolling in the complete training program. You will find details a little further on in this manual on how to enroll in the complete program if you want to go all the way.

If you do decide to continue on to the other units that follow this one, upon successful completion of your study of the course and all course work, you will earn your certificate in Wedding Floral Design.

You will then be fully prepared to begin designing flower arrangements for weddings, including: bouquets, boutonnieres, corsages, flower girl arrangements, centerpieces and other reception decorations, plus church and ceremony flowers like pew markers, altar arrangements - and more. You can use the wedding floral design skills you will learn in this course to gain employment as a wedding floral designer, or to start your own business designing flowers for the weddings of paying clients! Or if you're simply interested in wedding floral design for personal reasons or as a hobby, that's perfectly fine as well. By the time you're done the entire twelve unit course, you'll be able to design professional level wedding flowers that are sure to impress whomever you are designing for. Even if you are simply using this course to design professional quality flowers for your own wedding, you'll save yourself money, because in case you haven't noticed, wedding flowers will set your budget back a significant sum!

Learn From the Comfort and Convenience of Your Own Home

What's really terrific is that this course allows you to learn from the comfort and convenience of your own home, on your own schedule (this is known as distance education, distance learning or home study) so that you can fit your training into your lifestyle. You can even study in your pyjamas if you want! It will never disrupt your existing schedule or time commitments. You can learn at a pace which is comfortable to you. Do your learning when you feel able to focus – on any day of the week, at any time of the day or night that works for you – *not* on a schedule someone else sets.

Extensive Training Material

By the time you've taken all twelve units of the course, your extensive training lessons for the Wedding Floral Design course will consist of *more than 500 pages*, all written in an interesting and easy to follow manner, featuring step-by-step instructions, photographs, diagrams, and packed with all of the information you need for an exciting learning experience.

If after you complete this first unit of the course, you decide to continue on and enrol in the complete program, the additional eleven units of the course will promptly be shipped to your door following your enrolment in the course. They can be delivered to you all at once in one large shipment, or you have the option of having them delivered in monthly instalments.

If you decide to enrol in the full program, the course fee or monthly instalment payment includes not just the course units or lessons, but also the instructor, the assignments (no extra fees for tests like in some courses!), and your certificate (again, no additional certification fees as is common in courses of many types). Your course instructor is available to support and assist you with anything you need. If you have questions, need advice, or want further guidance, help is always just an email away. No need to travel to attend wedding floral design classes - you can do all your learning from the comfort of home. How perfect is that?

Weddings Are Big Business!

If you've recently been involved in planning, or *paying* for a wedding, you are likely well aware by now that WEDDINGS ARE BIG BUSINESS!

Every year a whopping $45 billion dollars is spent by consumers on their weddings. The wedding industry is a healthy, thriving, prosperous market to enter for anyone who has a genuine love of weddings, enjoys a glamorous environment, loves beautiful things, and likes dealing with people. It also offers some tremendous opportunity for anyone looking to establish a business of their own.

Have you looked at the cost of planning a wedding in your area recently?

Today's bride is spending more money than ever before in order to ensure that her wedding day – the single most important day of her life – is planned to complete perfection. And the cost of the average wedding is constantly going up, meaning brides are continually spending more and more on their weddings each year.

In the US and Canada, the average wedding back in 2002 came in at a cost of approximately $23,000. By 2015 the cost of the average wedding had jumped to over $30,000 - and many couples spend far in excess of that amount.

And it's not just in the US and Canada that weddings command such cash, in the United Kingdom, the average couple spent £14,500 in 2002 and that figured rose to £24,000 in 2015.

Big money is being spent on weddings in countries all around the world, and as such, there is always opportunity for wedding floral designers in the job market, or for wedding floral designers who want to operate their own businesses, either by working from home, or setting up shop in a retail location. .

Flowers play a major role in wedding décor, and also lend themselves to wedding fashion and style. Flowers are a significant focal point at any wedding. And so, the role of the wedding floral designer is an important one. So much so that it is quite likely that the bride will remember the person she selects to design her wedding flowers for many years beyond her big day. Flowers help the bride achieve that fairy tale effect which she has been dreaming of since she was a little girl. Surrounded by things of beauty and luxury on her wedding day, the bride is made to feel like a princess, if just for that one brief day of her life. As the floral designer, you will be instrumental in helping to create that feeling for her. What could be more exciting or rewarding?

As a wedding floral designer, you've got one of the best jobs in the world. You get to constantly surround yourself with people who are at the happiest points in their lives, and you will make an important contribution to one of the most memorable days they'll ever experience. When you have the opportunity to work in not one, but two glamorous fields – the *floral* industry *and* the *wedding* industry – you'll exist in a world of happiness, anticipation, excitement, prestige, glamour, beauty and romance.

This course will provide you with a foundation of knowledge to develop the skills to design wedding flowers beautifully and professionally – as a career, as a business, or if you prefer, simply as a pleasurable pass-time or hobby doing flowers for the weddings of friends and family. You can use the skills you acquire in this course for pleasure, to earn extra part time income, or turn them into a new career or business - you choose!

Once you've completed this course you'll impress everyone around you with your newly developed talent, skill, knowledge, and floral design abilities.

Every year, hundreds of students use The International Institute of Weddings training programs to successfully pursue their dreams within the wedding industry. Since 1999 students have told us that our extensive home study courses have changed their lives, opened up new doors of opportunity for them, and made it possible for them to fulfill their dreams.

Weddings are such an exciting field – always filled with fun and exciting new experiences – and we take great pride and satisfaction in giving our students the specialized knowledge and skills they need to enjoy a future doing something they love in the always glamorous wedding industry. We want to help you do the same;

we are committed to your success, and to providing you with a rewarding and enjoyable learning experience.

No Previous Floral Design Experience Required

With this one-of-a-kind course, no previous experience with floral design is required. We'll start you right at the beginning. And if you *do* have experience in floral design on an informal, self-taught, or hobby basis, this Wedding Floral Design Course will ensure that you learn the *proper* techniques, methods, and theory of professional floral design, to enable you to be *the best designer you can be.*

An Enjoyable Learning Experience

Whenever you're learning about something you love and are genuinely interested in, taking a course is fun – it's never boring, dull or tedious. So even if you were never a great student in school, you can expect it to feel a lot different as you go through the study units in this course. As you learn more and more, and you see your skills developing quickly, your excitement grows. And with that, your confidence in yourself as a designer will grow too.

Wedding Floral Design – Profitable and Enjoyable

Floral design is a fascinating art form which has its origins in ancient history – people have been enjoying floral design literally since the beginning of civilization. It's little wonder that humans have been drawn to the art of floral design and flower arranging for so very long – it instils a sense of relaxation, it's a wonderful creative outlet, and can be a rewarding, fulfilling, enjoyable way to spend one's time.

Many people enjoy floral design purely as recreation. But it can also be very profitable for those who choose to pursue it as a career or business, whether as a serious full time occupation, or simply to earn some extra spending money while doing something you really enjoy. For many, it is like living a dream to have the ability to earn great money while doing something you'd happily spend your own free time on.

When you indulge your creative instincts, it calms the soul, clears the mind, and lifts the spirit. By so intently focusing your attention on the design you are creating, you are taken into almost a meditative state, forgetting about life's other pressures. It's so satisfying to use your own creativity to achieve a beautiful end-result, and with that comes a rewarding sense of accomplishment every time – no matter how long you have been designing, or how many floral arrangements you have made in the past. And there's extra special feeling of satisfaction when you know the designs you are creating are for the single most important day of someone's life, their wedding day.

The Goal of This Course...

This course is made up of many distinct sections, each focusing on a specific area of wedding floral design. Each time you go through another section of the course, it's like you have taken another class. The wedding floral design classes that are spread out over the 12 units of the full course will teach you how to design wedding flowers *the right way* - using the proper techniques and methods. Our wedding floral design classes contained within the units will transform an amateur into professional wedding floral designer. When you have completed all the wedding floral design classes contained in the complete 12 unit course, you will know how to produce designs of professional quality.

One of the things people enjoy most about floral design is the creative process. However, every floral designer will tell you that a firm understanding of the recognized guidelines and fundamental principles of floral design is essential for the designer to have a solid foundation from which to spread her creative wings.

The goal of this course and the wedding floral design classes it contains is to demonstrate fascinating techniques, methods, principals and theories of floristry as they pertain specifically to wedding floral design, in addition to offering inspiration in the form of innovative and creative approaches and ideas. This is what leads to really *amazing looking*, professional designs.

Within the 12 units that make up the full course, you'll explore design theory so that, when combined with your creativity and imagination, this base of formalized knowledge will enable you to create arrangements which have wonderful structure, a universal sense of appeal, and deliver amazing visual impact – in other words, quality arrangements which look sensational. But don't let the word 'theory' make you 'creative types' uneasy. Floral design is first and foremost an art form, and we will treat it, appreciate it, and approach it as such. Therefore, although it is important to understand the theory of good design, this course is not about memorizing endless rules of design theory. After all, what is art if it isn't about expressing your own personal taste and sense of style, and allowing your eye to create a work which it naturally finds pleasing?

Behind every breathtakingly beautiful bridal bouquet or arrangement lies an understanding of some rather 'mechanical' procedures which you will learn in another unit of this course. For example, properly processing and conditioning flowers or greenery so that they remain at optimal freshness during their long hours at the center of attention is critically important in creating an exquisite design.

It is also essential to have solid knowledge of the proper methods of bouquet construction if you are to design bouquets which show well, are professional looking, and are durable. Having a firm understanding of the various wiring and taping techniques for wedding bouquets, corsages, boutonnieres and other arrangements will give your designs strong support and good shape, ensuring that they maintain the look you intended for them to have, and that they remain well assembled from the time they are delivered to the wedding right up until the moment the music stops playing and the last guest leaves. What an embarrassment it would be, to say the least, if the brides bouquet were to start falling apart at the wedding. It's happened far too many times to far too many brides due to poorly constructed designs put together by people with no knowledge of the proper techniques. This course will ensure you have a firm understanding of those proper design techniques.

An exceptional designer will also always want to pay very close attention to the *finishing details;* there are many possible ways to make use of finishing touches which can transform an ordinary bouquet into one which is absolutely awesome.

In one of the more advanced units of the course we'll teach you how to create *pretty stem wraps, lovely bouquet collars, and exquisite handle treatments –* because as we like to say here at The Institute of Weddings, when it comes to weddings, *the details make all the difference!*

The Tools and Knowledge You Need to Succeed

To be a wedding floral designer it is essential to have the technical knowledge and skill taught in this course. However, while some courses strive to make the art of floral design seem overly complicated, this course has been developed to do precisely the opposite. The objective of all the floral design classes contained in the 12 different units of this course is to show you how really simple all of the techniques, processes, methods, and procedures actually are once you understand them, and how very attainable the skills to become a proficient wedding floral designer are when they are presented in the right manner. With the instruction provided in this course, anyone with the desire to learn wedding floral design can be creating beautiful flowers for weddings in just a short time. We boil down all of the theory, techniques, methods and approaches so that they are easy to understand, to utilize, and to apply into your own design work.

Learn How to Re-Create Any Design

Better yet, the complete course will provide you with the solid foundation of knowledge and understanding to create designs of your own, and to have the ability to design the flowers you see in photos. With the fundamentals you will learn throughout the twelve units contained in the full course, you will never be dependent on someone else to provide you with instructions or 'recipes' for making floral arrangements. The complete program gives you the tools you need to be able to design independently. This is what it means to be a *real designer.*

Thinking of Starting Your Own Home Based Wedding Floral Design Business?

Once you have completed all of the units and lessons in the full 12-unit course, one option available to you will be to go into business as a wedding floral designer if you so choose. Our self-study training manual, *How to Start & Operate a Wedding Floral Business* is *an invaluable resource* for anyone who is interested in pursuing this path, and since 1999, has helped thousands of people just like you to establish their own wedding floral businesses, either working from the comfort of their own home, or opening storefront. It will pave the way for you to successfully, affordably, efficiently, and quickly establish your own business as a wedding floral designer. It will provide you with the specific and detailed information you need to know to become a major player in your area for the services you will offer.

If you already have a small business as a wedding floral designer, this business training manual provides you with strategic business knowledge to propel your business to heightened levels of success, to attract more customers, and to enable you to operate your business more effectively. It reveals the trade secrets, pricing formulas, marketing strategies and insider's information to bring you business and make you money.

And if you currently operate some other form of business within the wedding industry, the wedding floral business manual will show you how to successfully add wedding floral design services to your operation in order to significantly expand your base of revenue and provide the bride with a more extensive, full service shopping environment. More information on the Wedding Floral Business manual is available at the back of this book; it can be purchased at Amazon.com or it can be ordered directly from the Institute of Weddings website at www.instituteofweddings.com

Students of All Ages

Our course lessons and training materials are always written in an easy to understand, enjoyable, yet highly informative manner. So whether you are 18 or 81 years of age (and yes, we've had students at all ages and stages of life!), and everything in between, this course will be of benefit. All you need is a passion for flowers and weddings, and a genuine desire to learn. We'll take it from there!

Getting Started With Your Unit 1 Lessons

Are you ready to begin? Getting started is easy! Simply begin your study of Unit One of the course material by carefully reading through the lessons contained in this training manual. If anything seems unclear, stop and go through the material again to get a better understanding. It's a good idea to make notes along the way, or get out your highlighter pen to draw attention to important points.

If you want to earn your certificate for this course, you'll need to enroll in the full 12-unit training program by visiting www.instituteofweddings.com/enroll-now. After you have enrolled in the full program, at the end of Unit 6 it will be time to complete the mid-term exam. In the meantime, just focus on the lessons and enjoy what you are learning. The lessons will get more and more detailed as you go deeper into the course and you'll find yourself becoming more excited with each additional course unit you study as you feel your knowledge and skill set expanding. Once you have completed the study of all twelve units of this course, it will be time for the final exam. Upon successfully passing both the mid-term and final exam, you will earn your certificate in Wedding Floral Design.

There's lots of excitement ahead, but it all begins right now, by proceeding on to your study of the lesson material contained in this unit. Once you've completed Unit One, be sure to move right on to Unit Two by enrolling in the complete 12-unit course with as little delay as possible so you can keep the momentum of your learning experience going.

Ready? Then let's get started! Begin your study of the Unit 1 lesson material now.

In the complete course, you will learn:

As you can see from the detailed course outline below, we've packed a lot into the intensive twelve-unit Wedding Floral Design training program. We cover it all – it doesn't get more in-depth and thorough than this. By the time you have completed all 12 of the units in this extensive twelve unit program, you will be fully prepared as a wedding floral designer. You will have learned everything you need to know to design stunning flowers for weddings, including:

COURSE INTRODUCTION

The Evolution of Floral Design Throughout History

The Place of Flowers In Weddings

History of Wedding Floral Design: How, When, & Why it all Began

The Role of Flowers at Weddings Today

Flowers and Socio-Economic Status

Wedding Flowers and Cost

History of the Bridal Bouquet

The Bridal Bouquet & The Modern Wedding

The Role of the Wedding Floral Designer

Weddings By Month

Popular Wedding Flower Types

Popular Flowers For Weddings

Types of Lilies Commonly Used for Weddings

Types of Orchids Commonly Used for Weddings

Guidelines for Selecting Types of Flowers For Wedding Design Work

Seasonal Availability

Seasonal Design

Floriography

The Language & Meaning of Flowers

Incorporating the Language & Meaning of Flowers Into Wedding Floral Bouquet Design

DESIGN THEORY

The Elements of Design

Form

Line

Texture

Size

Space

Shape

Pattern

The Principals of Design

Balance

Contrast

Movement

Rhythm

Proportion

Scale

Dominance

Unity

Harmony

Color

Color in Wedding Floral Design

The Role of Color

Color Symbolism

Factors in Selecting Color

Color and Reception Flowers

Color Theory

FLOWER CLASSIFICATIONS IN DESIGN

Line Flowers

Form Flowers (Secondary or Focal Flowers)

Filler Flowers

Foliage Classifications In Design

Line Foliage

Form Foliage

Design Techniques

Basing

Layering

Grouping

Clustering

Zoning

Sequencing

Focal Point

Banding

Binding

Shadowing

Framing

Parallelism

Design Styles Which May Be

Utilized In Wedding Floral Design

Western Line

Mille de Fleur

Flemish

Crescent

Biedermeier

Waterfall

DESIGNING WITH SILK FLOWERS

Techniques

Methods

Tips

DESIGNING WITH FRESH FLOWERS

Processing & Conditioning Techniques For Fresh Flowers and Foliage

The Right Tools For the Job

Processing Stems

Removing Stamens

Cutting Stems

Crushing Stems

Filling Stems

Burning Stems

Boiling Stems

Pricking Stems

Processing Buddy Stems

Stripping Branches

Stripping Thorns

Stripping Leaves

Straightening Curvy Stems

Plunging Stems: Method I

Plunging Stems: Method II

Total Immersion

Proper Techniques for Inserting Stems Into Floral Foam

Working With Floral Tape

Tying Florist's Bows

Boutonnieres (Buttonholes)

Boutonniere

Construction Instructions

Corsages

Corsage Construction

The Five Basic Corsage Styles

Instructions for Basic Corsage Styles

Advanced Corsage Styles

Wrist Corsage or "Wristlet"

Tips for Boutonnieres and Corsages

BOUQUET CONSTRUCTION

Bouquet Design and Construction

The Two General Approaches

Size of the Bridal Bouquet

Bouquet Alternatives for Bridesmaids

Color and the Bridal Bouquet

Preparing to Design

Bouquet Design Instructions

Designing the Nosegay or Colonial Bouquet

The Classic Cascade

The Oval Bouquet

The Heart Bouquet

Designing the Wired Bouquet

STEM WRAPS AND BOUQUET COLLARS

Classic Ribbon and Bow Method

Square-End or Classic Method

Exposed-End Method

Collar Method

Finishing Details: Streamers

Finishing Details: Ballet Wrap

Table Centerpieces

Topiary Trees

Designing for the Flower Girl

Pomander

Attendants Baskets

The "Tossing" or "Throwaway Bouquet"

Container Arrangements

Methods for Securing Floral Foam to the Container

Ceremony Flowers

Flowers Greet the Guests

Adorn the Aisle

Highlight the Bride

The Alter: Focal Point Flowers

Enhance and Highlight

Complement the Location

Harmony Between Ceremony Site and Style of Floral Arrangements

Recommended Flowers for Church Arrangements

Recommended Colors for Church Arrangements

Working On Site

Pew Markers

DESIGN TECHNIQUES

Reception Flowers

Setting Up Flowers at the Reception Site

Centerpieces

Guidelines for Centerpiece Design

Popular Traditional Centerpiece Styles

High Construction

Centerpiece Construction Instructions

Wedding Cake Décor

General Guidance

Cake Top (Cake Topper)

CONSULTING WITH THE BRIDE

Decorative Techniques

Conceptualizing the Design

Basic Types of Flowers for Weddings

Comprehensive List of Supplies

Proper Care and Use of Floral Knifes

About Florist Wire

Storage Containers for Fresh Flowers

Floral Foam

Oasis Holders

Moss

Candles

Aesthetic Supplies

Designing With Fresh Florals

Where Our Fresh Flowers Come From

The Business of Commercial Flower Production

Seasonal Flowers

Obtaining Quality Flowers:

Sources of Supply

Examination and Selection of Fresh Flowers

Ordering Flowers

Taking Delivery of Flowers

Storing Fresh Flowers

Cataloguing Your Flowers

Sanitization and Fresh Flowers

The Fresh Floral Design Schedule

Considerations When Advising the Bride on Fresh Floral Selection

Other Considerations When Advising the Bride on Floral Selection

Getting Imaginative With Fresh Plant Materials

And still more....

In this study unit, you will learn:

Welcome to Unit 1 of this extensive twelve unit Wedding Floral Design Course by the International Institute of Weddings.

In this unit we take you through a fascinating introduction to the exciting world of wedding floral design.

Before you can dive into designing flowers for weddings, you need to have a good and broad understanding of the field of wedding floral design so that you come across as knowledgeable and competent when working with bridal clients, prospective employers and other wedding vendors.

The background knowledge you'll learn in this section will not only be interesting and fun to learn, it will lay a solid foundation for the design lessons that are to follow in the subsequent units of the course. Moreover, what you learn in this unit will increase your level of expertise and set you apart as a true professional as opposed to an amateur who has little back ground knowledge draw upon about the field of wedding floral design.

Here's what you are about to learn in Unit One:

The Evolution of Floral Design Throughout History

The Place of Flowers In Weddings

History of Wedding Floral Design: How, When, & Why it all Began

The Role of Flowers at Weddings Today

Flowers and Socio-Economic Status

Wedding Flowers and Cost

History of the Bridal Bouquet

The Bridal Bouquet & The Modern Wedding

The Role of the Wedding Floral Designer

Weddings By Month

Popular Wedding Flower Types

Popular Flowers For Weddings

Types of Lilies Commonly Used for Weddings

Types of Orchids Commonly Used for Weddings

Guidelines for Selecting Types of Flowers For Wedding Design Work

Seasonal Availability

Seasonal Design

Floriography

The Language & Meaning of Flowers

Incorporating the Language & Meaning of Flowers Into Wedding Floral Bouquet Design

Preface

The Love of Floral Design

It is fascinating to note that the art of floral design literally has its origins in antiquity. We know that people have enjoyed arranging flowers since the beginning of time because we find remnants of it as far back as history will take us. We've seen evidence of it on Egyptian tombs, Grecian urns, and in Roman Mosaics. And of course, throughout history, paintings have recorded man's interest in an intriguing variety of styles and forms of floral design.

It is little wonder that humans have been drawn to the art of arranging flowers for so very long; floral design is a *wonderfully relaxing* art. So much so that many people enjoy it simply as recreation. It's absolutely awesome, then, that it can also be *profitable* for those of us who apply our talents in order to pursue it as a career or business. To be able to earn an income by doing something you already love, something you would devote your free time to is nothing less than a true blessing, wouldn't you agree?

When an individual is driven by a genuine love of floral design, it soothes the soul, clears the mind, and lifts the spirit. By so intently focusing your attention on the design you are creating, you are taken into almost a meditative state, forgetting about other pressures, and using your creativity to achieve a wonderful end-result and a rewarding sense of accomplishment.

Experts in hypnosis tell us that the act of practicing an art such as floral design, in fact, actually places the designer in a hypnotic, trance-like state. If you become very relaxed, peaceful, and tranquil when you design (as happens for many designers), you are actually in a mild state of hypnosis which has resulted from focusing your mind so intently on something you enjoy. We find that wonderfully fascinating!

Like other forms of art, floral design has the ability to *translate*. Through this translation, floral design enables physical objects to create mood, evoke feeling, or establish an impression.

What is also so amazing about floral design is that, as with other art forms, a piece of the designer's personality is imbedded into every design. The designer leaves his or her own lasting imprint on everything he/she creates. If we give five designers an identical set of flowers, tools, and supplies to work with, they will each come up with their very own, very unique creations and interpretations. No two designs will ever be alike, because no two designers are alike. Every design created is as unique as its creator. This demonstrates the limitless possibilities in floral design, which so excites and inspires those of us who are smitten by this particular art form.

The Marriage of Creativity and Design Theory

There was a time when floral design was dictated by intimidating and rigidly prescribed formulas and rules for carefully arranging different shapes, textures, and colors into tightly constructed arrangements. With all the formulas and formal rules, floral design once more resembled science than art!

Fortunately, this art form has relaxed itself considerably over time, allowing today's designer a much higher level of creative expression. One of the most delicious things about floral design today is the inventiveness and freedom which is so much a part of it.

However, a firm understanding of the recognized guidelines and fundamental principals of floral design must still be mastered in order to provide the designer with a solid foundation from which to spread her/his creative wings.

This course will explore design theory so that, when combined with your own creativity and imagination, this base of formalized knowledge will be translated into arrangements which have good structure, a universal sense of appeal, and the ability to deliver maximum visual impact.

But don't let the word 'theory' make you 'creative types' uneasy! Floral design *is* first and foremost an *art* form, and it should be treated, appreciated, and approached as such. Therefore, although it is important to understand the theory of good design, this course is *not* about memorizing endless rules of design theory. After all, what is art if it isn't about *expressing* your own personal taste and sense of style, and allowing your eye to create a work which it *naturally* finds pleasing?

Instead, the goal of this course is to demonstrate fascinating techniques of floristry and floral design *as they pertain specifically to wedding floral design*, in addition to offering inspiration in the form of many innovative, helpful, and creative approaches or ideas.

Behind every breathtakingly beautiful bridal bouquet or arrangement lies an understanding and implementation of some rather 'mechanical' procedures which you will also learn in this course. For example, although appropriately processing and conditioning flowers, so that they remain at optimal freshness during their long hours at the center of attention, may be one of the *least* time consuming tasks, it is also one of the most critically important steps in creating an exquisite design.

It is also essential to have solid knowledge of the proper methods of bouquet construction if you are to design bouquets which not only show well, but which have durability. Having a firm understanding of the various wiring and taping techniques for wedding bouquets will give your designs strong support and good shape, ensuring that they are able to maintain the look you intended for them to have, and remain well assembled from the time they are delivered to the moment the music stops playing and the last guest leaves.

And there's more. After planning the overall design of a bouquet or floral arrangement, an exceptional designer will always want to pay very close attention to the finishing details; there are many possible extra touches which can transform an ordinary bouquet into one which is *extraordinary*. For example, giving special attention to the bouquet's handle by way of pretty treatments of ribbon, fabric wraps, or a beautiful collar is just as important in perfectly completing the look of a bouquet as it might be for the bride to add an exquisite pair of earrings to give her wedding day attire the perfect finishing touch.

At any wedding it is the attention to the smallest of wedding details which will make the longest lasting impression - not only on the bride, but on her wedding guests as well. This holds particularly true where floral design is concerned.

For centuries, wedding flowers have had the ability to stimulate the senses and to parlay grand emotions and great expectations. Applying your imagination and creativity into the designs you create will produce works of art that will leave a wonderful imprint on the minds of all who take them in with their eyes. When your job has been done well, your floral designs have the ability to speak to the soul, as well as the senses. What an awesome thing to be able to do!

To be a wedding floral designer it is essential to have the technical knowledge and skill taught in this course. But creativity and imagination are also a must. Ultimately you must have the ability to marry the two.

While some courses strive to make the art of floral design seem overly complicated and complex, this course has been developed to do precisely the opposite. The objective is to show you how really simply it all can be boiled down, and how very attainable the skills to become a proficient wedding floral designer truly are when they are presented in the right manner.

We intend for you to have fun learning about the fascinating field of wedding floral design, and to enjoy the excitement that comes with acquiring the new skills, abilities, knowledge and techniques you will quickly gain as you study this course.

Specializing in Flowers for Weddings

Never before has there been a home study course specifically designed to train the student to specialize in wedding floral design. All of the lessons in this course are focused towards providing you with a highly specialized level of knowledge about flowers for weddings – *exclusively weddings*.

Weddings are one of the single most important and monumental events in the human experience. And flowers play an important role in that event. As such, it makes sense that the individual entrusted to create flowers for one's wedding should have a very focused level of knowledge and training in this area. As time goes on, and you become more practiced and experienced at designing flowers exclusively for weddings, that knowledge and training will translate into some powerful expertise. Brides will value the fact that you devote yourself exclusively to designing flowers for weddings, and only weddings.

In the past, when an individual was attracted to the area of wedding floral design, they had no option but to invest their time and money into more generalized floral design training programs. This meant they were spending their money and effort on courses that taught them a lot about areas they were *not* interested in and did not intend to use, and *not enough* about the one area which actually attracted them, and which they intended to specialize in. That's not an effective approach.

This course won't waste valuable pages, or your time, money, and effort forcing you to learn concepts, techniques, methods, or principles which have no application in wedding floral design, and which will therefore bore you, curb your enthusiasm, and never again be used by you. If you want to focus on floral design within the wedding industry, you don't want to be forced to invest time and money to learn how to design casket sprays for funerals or get-well arrangements for hospitals.

Instead, our focus – and yours - will be solely on weddings, *weddings,* and *more* weddings! This course will provide you with extensive background information on weddings as they are related to floral design, and it will teach you the concepts of floral design as they apply to weddings. Upon completion, you will have learned all of the fundamentals and basics of wedding floral design, including design techniques, principals, theory, methods, and approaches.

We will provide you with step by step instructions that will get you started in creating your wedding floral designs. But better yet, we'll teach you the basic principles and approaches so that you need not rely on the instructions or 'recipes' of others, for that would only limit your ability as a designer. Instead, we will give you the knowledge and tools to create limitless designs all on your own, by mastering the basic techniques and concepts. Then, combined with your own common sense, creativity, and imagination, you'll have the ability to independently recreate designs you have seen in photos, and to continually create new ones all of your own.

Even if you have taken other floral design courses in the past, this one will be invaluable in furthering your knowledge of weddings, so that you may move towards wedding floral specialist status. If you are self taught or a hobbyist, this course will ensure that you learn the proper techniques and methods of wedding floristry, and that you acquire the training and credential you need to charge professional prices for the work you do. And if you have never worked with flowers before, this course is just right for you as well – we'll start you out at the very beginning and guide you every step of the way.

If you are a newcomer to the wedding industry, we bid you a warm welcome. The personal satisfaction you experience as you work with couples in planning the day they have been dreaming of for their entire lives is likely to surpass even your greatest expectations. We wish you tremendous success in your future as a wedding floral designer!

Introduction

Since ancient times, flowers have held an important place in weddings. They have been used to communicate meaning and to express symbolism throughout the ages.

As weddings evolved over time into increasingly more elaborate affairs, so too did the flowers which were such a key component to these events. As bridal gowns became more extravagant, bridal bouquets followed the same path.

Today, at the start of a whole new century, flowers remain as important as ever in the modern day wedding celebration and often represent a significant percentage of the wedding budget.

As a couple begins their new life together, the flowers that surround them on their wedding day symbolize life itself. Flowers also represent the growth and change that exists over the life of the couple's relationship, and the nurturing and care any marriage demands.

Flowers play a major role in wedding décor, and lend themselves to wedding fashion. They provide a significant focal point at any wedding.

And so, the role of the wedding floral designer is an important one. So much so that it is quite likely that the bride will remember the person she selects to design her wedding flowers for many years beyond her big day. Flowers help the bride achieve that fairy tale effect which she has been dreaming of since she was a little girl. Surrounded by such things of beauty and luxury on her wedding day, the bride is made to feel like a princess, if just for that one brief day of her life. As the floral designer, you will be instrumental in helping to create that feeling for her.

The work of a floral designer is, then, very meaningful and rewarding. You will play a crucial role in what will be the most important day in the lives of the people you design for. Your work will always be at "center-stage", seen and admired potentially by thousands of people over the life-span of your career as a designer.

At any single wedding alone, typically speaking, anywhere from one-hundred to four-hundred sets of eyes will take in the beauty of your creations (statistics indicate that the *average* wedding today has 250 guests). With the growing popularity today of fresh flower preservation for wedding bouquets, as well as the trend towards the use of permanent botanicals (silk and dried flowers), your designs may live on to be gazed at and admired for many years after the event itself - an ever present reminder of the wonderful occasion. They will undoubtedly stir the minds of those who possess them to recall some very precious memories.

As a wedding floral designer, you've got one of the best jobs in the world. You get to constantly surround yourself with people who are at the happiest points in their lives, and you will make a contribution to the most memorable day of their lives. Because you have chosen to be a designer in both the floral industry *and* the wedding industry, you'll exist in a world of happiness, anticipation, excitement, glamour, creativity, beauty and romance. For many of those who opt to pursue this as a career or business, this is truly *the* dream job.

This course will provide you with a foundation of knowledge to develop the skills to design wedding florals beautifully, skillfully, and professionally. Once you have completed this course, you can consider going into business as a wedding floral designer if you so choose.

Our very popular self-study training manual, *How to Start and Operate a Wedding Floral Business* is available for those who wish to pursue this path, and it will pave the way for you to successfully, affordably, efficiently, and quickly establish your own business as a wedding floral designer (visit www.instituteofweddings.com for more information on this training manual). It will provide you with the specific and detailed information you need to become a major player in your area as a wedding floral designer.

If you already have a small business as a wedding floral designer, *How to Start and Operate a Wedding Floral Business* will provide you strategic business knowledge to propel your business to heightened levels of success, to attract more customers, and to enable you operate your business more effectively.

And if you currently operate some *other* form of business within the wedding industry, the wedding floral business training manual will show you how to successfully add wedding floral design services to your business in order to significantly expand your base of revenue and provide the bride with a more extensive, full service shopping environment.

Once you have completed this course and have the ability to use your newfound knowledge and skills to turn your interest in floral design and weddings into a viable career or business, it won't be long before you are the envy of many. How many people have the opportunity to earn an income doing what they love, in a glamorous industry like this one, perhaps even from the comfort and convenience of home?

Working from home is a very viable option for the wedding floral designer, and in fact, we encourage you to seriously consider it for the many advantage it offers: Low overheard, minimal operational expenses, zero commuting time, the ability to be home with young children if applicable, the ability to involve other members of the household in a 'family business', the ability to more efficiently manage one's time, tax advantages, and then there is the *comfort* factor - put simply, it's incredibly comfortable to work from home!

Today, with the increasing popularity of telecommuting in the modern world, its becoming extremely common for people to earn their living right from home, so you needn't fret that you will be taken less seriously as a home based wedding floral designer. In fact, the home based operation is quite suitable for wedding floral designers, as it provides an intimate, comfortable and more personal environment for the client to meet with you, and brides in particular respond very favorably to that.

Perhaps you may have your sights set on opening a shop once you have completed your wedding floral training. That, of course, is an equally wonderful option. It all comes down to each individual's personal preference, and to whatever will suit your lifestyle best. The important thing to note is that your options will be open, and you will be free to proceed in the manner that works best for you.

In either case, once you are ready to establish a business in wedding floral design, *How to Start and Operate a Wedding Floral Business* will be an invaluable tool in successfully translating your new wedding floral design skills and knowledge into the pride, prestige, and satisfaction of owning a profitable business of your own. Visit the Institute of Weddings website (www.instituteofweddings.com) for more information.

You are very fortunate. Many people dream of being able to earn an income doing something they truly love, perhaps even in a business of their own, but few will ever acquire the skills or abilities to make that dream a reality. You've made the decision to take control of your destiny and go after your dream, and now you are taking the steps necessary to make it happen through the pursuit of the specialized knowledge found in this course. Soon you will be able to surround yourself with beautiful things and happy people while earning an income in the process.

Are you excited to get on with the lessons in this new learning experience? Then *lets do it!*

[This page intentionally left blank]

Unit 1: Overview

The Evolution of Floral Design Throughout History

The art of floral design literally has its origins in antiquity. People have used flowers to beautify their environments quite literally since the beginning of time. Man's appreciation for the beauty of flowers is evidenced throughout the ages, and we find remnants of man's interest in floral arts as far back as history will take us. We have seen it depicted on Egyptian tombs, on Grecian urns, and in Roman Mosaics. And of course, throughout history, paintings and sculptures have recorded the beauty of floral designs in an intriguing variety of forms and styles.

In the earliest examples of floral design, people took their lessons and ideas form Mother Nature herself. Tall arrangements of flowers were inspired by trees, while round arrangements were modeled after bushes.

It is fascinating to think that this art, which today provides us with such an enjoyable means of spending our time, and allows many of us to earn a good living, actually has its roots in ancient history. How intriguing that it has withstood the tests of time through the ages in order to be passed along to us to enjoy, and sometimes even earn our livings from, in the sophisticated world in which we live today.

Your love of floral design connects you to the past. It is important to have an appreciation for all of the designers who came before you and developed the techniques we use today, perfecting and refining them over the years, to be passed along to us in their current form. We have inherited so much from them.

Following is a brief but very interesting look at how the history of floral design can be traced back to the origins of time.

3000 – 332.B.C.

Egyptian tombs give us a glimpse into the manner in which flowers were enjoyed during the period of 3000 – 332.B.C. Inscriptions and paintings in the tombs depict: vases of flowers in ceremonial proceedings (the earliest versions of today's alter arrangements!); women wearing blooms as corsages; women wearing blooms in their hair; bowls of buds and blooms on banquet tables (the earliest table centerpieces!).

Egyptian Mummies have even been uncovered with the dried remains of garlands, wreaths, and floral headpieces adorning them.

600 B.C – 325 A.D

Greek and Roman architecture and artifacts from 600 B.C – 325 AD depict people wearing wreaths and garlands made from a variety of plant materials, including one particular type which has persevered through the ages as a favorite to this day – *ivy*. Mosaics show baskets filled with combinations of different flowers.

Roses are believed by scientists to have been flourishing on this earth for 30 million years (rose fossils that have been carbon dated some 35 million years old have been found in the US states of Montana and Oregon), but they are first seen in the art of the Greeks and Romans from this period.

1400 A.D – 1600 A.D

Artwork from the Renaissance Period (1400 A.D – 1600 A.D) depicts considerably more elaborate floral designs and adornments, with heavy use as décor in residential dwellings and churches. This period was very influential in the way we use floral arrangements in décor today at celebrations, ceremonies, and within our homes. Cut flowers used in tall spray bouquets and small, tight bunches of cut flowers emerge for the first time in artwork from this era. Also seen for the first time are flowers arranged in specific patterns, as opposed to the random scatterings which predated them.

The 17th Century

Dutch artwork from the 17th century makes it clear that floral design had become a true art form by this period, much resembling the way we continue to arrange flowers today. In paintings we see lush, lavish, full designs thoughtfully arranged and displayed in large vases. Also apparent is careful attention to proportion, form, color, mass and line.

The Victorian Era (1830 –1901)

The Victorian era (1830 –1901) was a period of industrialism and romance. Prosperity was dramatically on the rise during this time and people indulged in gorgeous arrangements of flowers to decorate their homes, as well as to express their love and affection in personal relationships.

An interesting thing happened in this marriage of industrialism and romance – the *silk flower* was born. Real silk was fashioned to reflect the beauty of flowers, and these silk flowers rapidly became popular for use in floral design. As they became increasingly popular they went into mass production which, of course, continues to this day.

The Place of Flowers In Weddings

As a wedding floral designer, it is necessary for you to have knowledge of the background and history of the field in which you work. So let is start with a brief look at the history flowers in weddings, from the beginning of time to the present.

By understanding where the traditions pertaining to the use of flowers originated, you will acquire a higher level of enlightenment regarding the work that you do. This will put you in a better position to design for the bride in a way which incorporates meaning and relevancy into her wedding flowers. The ability to knowledgeably answer questions pertaining to the background and significance of flowers with regards to weddings will help establish you as an educated professional and specialist in the field.

History of Wedding Floral Design:
How, When, & Why it all Began

Since ancient Roman times, flowers have had an important place in weddings. You might find it amusing to know that the use of flowers at weddings originally stemmed from *superstition* and the belief that they would drive away evil spirits that threatened to spoil the wedding day. The very first brides known in history wore little bunches of herbs tucked beneath their veils out of the belief that the purity of the herbs would successfully ward off such evil spirits.

The practice of having the bridesmaids carry bouquets also began out of the fear of evil spirits. The earliest bridesmaid bouquets consisted of odoriferous bunches of herbs and garlic - the first nosegays - with the idea that the purity of the herbs, combined with the pungent odor of garlic, would scare away any ill intending spirits.

The same logic lies behind the origin of the practice of having the groom and his attendants wear boutonnieres (known among our UK students as 'buttonholes'). As you are probably gathering by this point, the first boutonnieres consisted of a sprig of herb that was pinned on the groom to keep away evil.

As time went on, symbolism began to replace superstition where wedding flowers were concerned. It became tradition for brides to carry branches of orange blossoms, plucked from orange trees, on the wedding day as a symbol of purity and a wish for abundance, because the orange tree is the only plant which bears both the flower and the fruit at the same time.

The Role of Flowers at Weddings Today

Throughout the centuries, the tradition of incorporating flowers into every wedding has evolved to such a point that, to this day, flowers have a predominant place throughout the entire wedding festivities. The bride and her bridesmaids carry bouquets; flower girls carry baskets of blooms or petals; the groom, ushers, best man, groomsmen, page boys, fathers, and grandfathers wear boutonnieres; the mothers and grandmothers wear corsages; and other honored guests are often presented with flowers to wear as well.

Flowers also feature prominently in wedding day décor, of course.

The ceremony site is usually adorned with beautiful floral arrangements placed on either side of the alter, and pew markers are also frequently designed to include flowers.

At the reception, flowers serve as important focal points and have the ability to transform an uninteresting, even un-welcoming empty room into one of beauty and festiveness. Individual reception tables are appointed with floral centerpieces and the head table may be decorated with floral garlands. A garland of flowers may encircle the wedding cake and sometimes the cake itself is embellished with fresh or silk flowers and topped with a specially designed floral arrangement.

When one considers the number of hours guests will spend at the reception, gazing around the room, the importance of carefully considered, well designed floral arrangements cannot be diminished.

Flowers have always played such a highly important role in weddings because of the strong symbolism and meaning which is attached to them. Flowers do not exist in the modern day wedding merely because they look pretty and add the necessary decorative touches to such an event. The role of flowers goes far deeper than that. However, today, all too often the *significance* of flowers at the wedding may be lost or over looked.

For centuries, flowers have provided a well-utilized means of communicating love and romance, and thus have become symbolic of both. Individual flowers carry with them their own meaning and language, known within the industry as *floriography*. Even today, certain flowers are often incorporated into weddings based on the precise symbolism they hold and the meaning they represent, just as was the norm in centuries past.

Flowers, in fact, represent life itself, and thus, are highly appropriate and meaningful on the day when a young couple has chosen to begin a new life together as husband and wife.

Sometimes flowers are chosen for weddings as a reflection of the bride's own personality or as a significant hint of some aspect to the couple's history. A bride may choose to surround herself with yellow roses on her wedding day because this is, and has always been, her favorite flower. The significance of little white daisies everywhere at a wedding could very well be tied to the couple's first date, when the young man hand-picked a small bouquet of white daisies for his young lady as they walked along a stream at sunset.

Flowers and Socio-Economic Status

And lastly in our discussion of the role of flowers in weddings is the fact that flowers have always represented luxury, abundance, and lavishness. Since the earliest of days, surrounding the couple with flowers on their wedding day expressed a desire and wish for the newlyweds to have everything they would ever need, and to achieve much prosperity.

Over the course of history, the level of extravagance put into flowers at weddings has often been used as a measure of a family's wealth. Today, while it is considered somewhat socially incorrect to focus on a family's material worth, the fact remains that flowers will typically be more elaborate and in greater abundance at the weddings of those who are financially wealthier, than at those who are less so.

Flowers have always been associated with luxury. Regardless of whether the blooms are fresh or silk, flowers continue to have this association. And like so many other elements of a bride's wedding day, flowers allow her a luxury, on this one day out of her entire life, in which she may not otherwise be able to indulge. Flowers contribute greatly to the fantasy of being 'princess for a day', which is what being a bride is all about. She has met her prince and has found her fairy tale romance, and just before they slip off into the sunset, they partake in a gala ball to celebrate the love they have found in each other. All eyes are upon her, upon them. She in her flowing white gown, he in his dashing black tie and tails. There is food, there is wine, there is laughter and music, and there are the flowers. Flowers, flowers, everywhere.

And then, of course, they live happily every after...

Wedding Flowers and Cost

And where precisely does *cost* factor into all of this? Quite significantly, indeed. According to statistics, the bride will spend 5.8% of her total wedding budget on flowers and the services of a professional floral designer. Therefore, with the average wedding today totaling over $30,000 (US and Canada) in expenditures, the substantial sum spent for flowers is, on average, in excess of $1,000.

Designing to Suit the Budget

Sometimes a design may have to be adjusted to suit a bride's more limited budget. To accomplish this there are many things you can alter:

- the size of the arrangement
- the types of flowers used (substitute less exotic flowers, or use flowers that are in season instead imported flowers
- the quantity of flowers used (consider going heavier with filler material to decrease the number of focal flowers required)
- other props or materials used in the design (look for less expensive container options, etc)

History of the Bridal Bouquet

The very first bridal bouquet emerged in medieval times. It was the *nosegay* - tiny hand-tied bunches of flowers, originally herbs.

The Victorian era brought the emergence of the *tussie mussie*, a larger round bouquet of flowers usually encircled by fern leafs. The tussie mussie was distinguished by the silver, cone shaped holder which held the stems of the flowers.

The tussie mussie eventually evolved into the *cascade* towards the end of the Victorian era. Historically, the cascade was an all white bouquet which trailed almost to the bride's ankles.

The next style of bouquet to emerge appeared in the 1930s and was known as *Art Deco*. The style of bridal apparel for the day featured very sleek lines. In keeping with that, the bridal bouquet was sleek in it's design as well. Simple arrangements of sleek flowers such as calla lilies, or sometimes simply one individual long stemmed calla lily, made the bridal bouquet.

Since that time, like the trend in men's ties, bridal bouquets have changed in style and size to reflect the given economic situation of the day. In times of great economic prosperity, bouquets have been large and elaborate. When the economy turned less robust, bouquets were scaled down in size and detail.

Throughout history, bouquet styles have also changed with, and been influenced by, the evolution of the wedding gown. As the wedding gown became more elaborate over time, so too did the bridal bouquet.

And lastly, the style of bouquets throughout the years has been influenced by the mood of the time. As an example, in the early 1970s, bunches of wild flowers were popular for bridal bouquets, in keeping with the more relaxed, far less formal mood of that era. In the 1980's when glamour ruled once again, we saw more elaborate designs, as well as more sophisticated flower types.

The Bridal Bouquet & The Modern Wedding

Now that we've taken a look at the history of the bridal bouquet, what dictates the style of bouquet in *this* day and age?

Today, 'rules' about wedding bouquets have relaxed to the point where they have become almost non-existent. The bride today can essentially chose whatever style of bouquet she feels is most expressive of her personality, her own sense of style, and/or her wedding theme.

The guidelines for bouquet choice today are basic and simple – the bouquet style should be suitable to the style of wedding, the style of her gown, and her own physical stature. Where color traditionally was limited to white for wedding flowers, today's modern bride has the entire color spectrum to chose from – anything from the palest of pastels, to the most vivid and vibrant hues.

The Role of the Wedding Floral Designer

The wedding floral designer plays an important role in the wedding planning process. We have already discussed the importance of flowers in a wedding and the focal point which they create. The bride will look to you, her floral designer, to help her achieve her fairytale vision. She will rely on you to make that vision a reality. She will turn to you to help create any particular mood or atmosphere she is striving to achieve for her wedding.

In return, you will be rewarded by having the pleasure of working with people who are at one of the happiest points in their lives; where smiles and laughter are present in great abundance. You will have the honor of being trusted with assisting in what is very likely to be the most important and memorable day in your clients' lives. You will have the privilege of applying your creativity to help make the bride's wedding dreams a reality.

The bride will look to you for your creativity, talent, skill, technique, experience, imagination, and vision in designing the flowers of her dreams. She expects that you will not only know how to put together a look which is visually appealing, but that you will also be able to offer creative design suggestions and be able to advise her on the durability of flowers, the suitability of the flowers she is interested in, and the fragrance of flowers (if applicable). She will also depend on you to guide her in choosing flowers which best suit her budget from a cost perspective.

Also expected of the wedding floral designer is a strong level of professionalism, responsibility, organization, and competence, in addition to excellent interpersonal skills. In order to win the bride's confidence and gain her business, you will need to exhibit these qualities when meeting with her. The bride must feel comfortable and at ease with you - you must be pleasant for her to work with. Also very important, the bride must feel confident that she is able to depend on you when involving you in something so important as her wedding plans - and you must not let her down. It is essential that the flowers be designed as discussed with the bride in your consultation with her, and that they be delivered on time. There is no room for error or deviation from plan when the day people have been dreaming of all their lives is concerned.

Most bridal consultants and wedding experts advise brides to deal with a floral designer who *specializes* in weddings. The fact that you are choosing to specialize exclusively in the bridal segment of floral design will work very much in your favor and will create a very good selling point, niche, and competitive advantage for your service.

There are different levels of service a wedding floral designer can choose to offer. You will need to decide where you want to position yourself in this respect. Some wedding floral designers limit themselves strictly to designing bouquets, corsages, boutonnieres, and *spatial arrangements* like those for the alter and table centerpieces, while others choose to expand their role into that of complete wedding decor designer, specializing in creating a 'total environment' in even the most mundane of places.

In the case of the latter, you would work with the bride in designing and decorating the wedding as a whole, even if that means going slightly beyond the realm of floral design where required. You might be called upon to help create a visual theme for the wedding, and to put an entire look or concept together. You might, therefore, need to be involved in everything from designing the centerpieces to selecting the table linens, napkins, etc. - perhaps right down to decorative details as miniscule as the napkin rings, in fact. This can be great fun!

If you define yourself strictly as a wedding floral designer, you'll probably stick a little more closely to the business of bouquets and boutonnieres, and basic spatial arrangements. Once you venture off into the overall design of the wedding details, you are taking on more the role of a wedding planner or wedding stylist as opposed to that of floral designer.

Today, there is rapidly growing interest and demand among bridal consumers for the services of wedding coordinators. Many wedding floral designers are realizing that it is a logical 'next step' and an excellent opportunity for their businesses to expand into the area of wedding coordination, thereby taking their businesses to newer and higher heights while elevating the level of service they are able to offer their clients.

Many wedding florists find themselves naturally drawn to the area of wedding planning and wedding styling, out of their passion for weddings, the excitement which accompanies them, their love of romance and beautiful things, and their eye for detail. It is, in many ways, a natural progression for many floral designers to involve themselves in wedding planning and styling. Wedding planners may be called upon to get their hands into *all* areas of wedding planning, whereas wedding stylists focus on the visuals and the aesthetics of the wedding.

Professional wedding planning is a field which has grown enormously over the last decade as more and more couples discover the practical advantages that professional wedding planners can offer them. These advantages include convenience, the ability to save money on wedding costs, to save time, and to enjoy the wedding planning experience more, with less stress. With a properly qualified wedding planner on their team, couples often save more than enough money to cover the wedding planner's fee. So although wedding planners were once viewed as a 'status symbol', hired only by the elite, today more and more 'average' couples are using their services. In fact, statistics show that well over 50% of all couples today use a wedding planner at some point during their wedding planning process.

If you are considering an expansion of your wedding floral business to include professional wedding planning or styling, proper training is essential. For nearly twenty years, The International Institute of Weddings has been a well recognized leader in the provision of professional training and certification for wedding planners, offering some of the most thorough, comprehensive, practical, effective, and highly respected training for wedding planners available anywhere in the world, through convenient home-study. Used internationally by newcomers to the field, as well as by seasoned wedding planners seeking to perfect their abilities, every year since 1999, the course has successfully enabled hundreds of wedding planners to successfully develop their businesses. The International Institute of Weddings also offers the only training and certification program anywhere in the world for professional wedding stylists. For course information, you may visit the following websites:

- weddingplannercourse.com
- certifiedweddingstylist.com
- instituteofweddings.com

Assuming you do stick strictly to wedding floral design, there are still different levels of involvement which you may choose to take. This will depend to a certain extent on how you define your business and which particular market you are catering to.

For example, some floral designers find that the bulk of their customers call upon them simply for bouquets, boutonnieres, corsages, and flower girl baskets - the bare basics. Such customers may be slightly more budget constrained and often choose to handle items such as centerpieces on a do-it-yourself basis. Other florists may find that in addition to those basic items, they are typically expected to design "spatial" items such as alter arrangements and centerpieces for their clients as well. And still other floral designers report that their typical client requires them to go yet another step farther by designing creations such as cake flowers, table garlands, chair embellishments, floral archways, and so forth.

Precisely where you fit in will depend greatly on where your own personal interests, talents and creative abilities lie, how you market yourself, and the particular *demographics* of your area. The term demographics refers to the 'profile' of the market which you are serving, and is based on a number of factors such as the economic background, age group, and social make up of the area you are serving as a whole.

Thus, if you live in a small rural area which may be somewhat less affluent, you likely won't find yourself being called upon very frequently to design as lavishly as you might if you were based in, for example, The Hamptons or Palm Beach. However, you may still find that you can create quite a nice business for yourself doing simply the standard bouquets, corsages and boutonnieres which the clients in your area inevitably require. You may not have the opportunity to exercise your creativity by designing lavish and extravagant arrangements, but there is much to be said for recognizing who your market is and then focusing on giving it what it wants and needs, and there is still plenty of room for creative expression in that.

The key is that the precise level of service you offer must fit the market you are in. You can't sell ice to Eskimos, nor can you sell sand in the desert. A key element to your success as a wedding floral designer lies in recognizing *who* your market *is*, and then give it what it really *does* have need for.

Weddings By Month

Some people think of weddings as a "seasonal" business. After all, most brides prefer to have their weddings in the warm weather months of spring or summer. However, this does not imply by any means that the wedding floral designer can expect to take the rest of the year off.

A wedding may *take place* during the popular month of June, but for that occur, the bride-to-be had to book the services of her floral designer, plan her flowers, and place her order many months prior.

Weddings are being *planned* all year long, and while you may notice that you are busier at certain times of the year than you are at others, you will, without question, find that there is plenty of business to be had year-round.

As a wedding professional, you need to have a good handle on which months of the year tend to be the peak months for weddings. The break down is as follows:

Month	Percentage of Weddings
January	5.5%
February	5.5%
March	7.2%
April	7.9%
May	9.5%
June	11.9%
July	9.5%
August	9.6%
September	9.4%
October	8.5%
November	7.2%
December	8.3%

Popular Wedding Flower Types

There are a variety of flower types which are most popular for use in weddings. Of course, at the top of this list are roses, frequently embellished with baby's breath and ivy in bridal bouquets. Carnations and lilies are also very popular choices. As a designer, you may chose to work mostly with these types of blooms, or you may opt to be a little more adventuresome in terms of the types of flowers you will design with, perhaps exploring the area of more exotic flowers in your designs.

Other popular options for bridal flowers exist as well; below you will find a complete list of popular flower types for use at weddings, along with a brief description of each type.

Types of Flowers Commonly Used for Weddings

Roses Available in an amazingly large variety of colors and shades. Buds, as well as open flowers work well in wedding flower design. Two common sizes: standard size and 'Sweetheart' roses, which are smaller and daintier than the standard.

Carnations   Available in a wide variety of color and shade choices, and sometimes come in multicolored varieties.

Tulips Popular spring garden flower. Available in a good selection of colors.

Baby's Breath Tiny white flowers, commonly used as an embellishment flower. Frequently partnered with roses or carnations.

Ivy   Green, trailing, heart shaped vine, very popular for use in weddings and particularly the bridal bouquet as it is a strong symbol of fidelity.

Daisies   Yellow and white are the most common colors, however, colors such as blue, mauve, pink and purple are popular as well. Very appropriate for a simple or country style wedding.

Gerbera Daisies   Oversized daisies, frequently in bright colors. Popular when combined with carnations in bridesmaid bouquets.

Lilies   See below

Orchids   See below

Stephanotis   Very common in bridal bouquets, especially the cascading type. Very small, white star shaped flowers with a very deep throat. Fresh Stephanotis sometimes has a tendency to yellow in extreme heat, therefore, silks offer a definite advantage.

Freesia   Commonly used as a substitute for stephanotis. A lovely tiny flower available in white, yellow, red, and purple.

Types of Lilies Commonly Used for Weddings

Alstroemeria   Tiny, miniature lilies available in a wide range of colors, and often in multi-color varieties

Calla Lilies   Large, long tubular shaped white flowers on thick stalks with long shiny leaves. Very similar in appearance to Peace Lilies.

Star Gazers   Striking, large star shaped flowers of deep pink with white markings and large protruding stamen.

Oriental Lilies Large star shaped lilies in solid colors (red, orange, yellow, pink, white), of which white is most popular for weddings.

Lily-of-the-Valley   Clusters of tiny white blooms resembling little bells.

Many varieties of lilies, including Calla, Star Gazer, and Lily-of-the-Valley are enormously expensive when purchased fresh, making silks a very good choice for brides desiring such flowers - particularly those to whom budget is a factor.

Types of Orchids Commonly Used for Weddings

Japhet These large orchids feature an all-over curly edge and frequently have yellow throats.

Cymbidium   Smaller than the Japhet and featuring the curly edge only towards the center of the flower.

Dendrobium   Sprays of miniature orchids which are often used in trailing design pieces, but may be used individually as well.

Phalaenopsis White round-edged orchids featuring reddish throats. Because fresh Phalaenopsis are not very durable, silks are a very good choice for the bride desiring this type of orchid among her wedding flowers.

Guidelines for Selecting Types of Flowers For Wedding Design Work

There are a number of different factors which should be taken in to account when selecting the types of flowers used in the bridal bouquet. These include:

- the season in which the wedding will occur
- the style of the wedding itself
- the location and time of day the wedding
- the sentimental aspects of flowers
- the personality of the bride
- the theme of the wedding
- the budget

Capturing the Essence of the Season

When choosing flowers, an inspired designer will strive to select those which will capture the essence of the season in which the wedding will occur so as to reflect the color and mood of the time.

Spring Weddings

For instance, spring may call for softer colors and subtle scents, while summer demands hot, vibrant, or startling colors.

Fall Weddings

In the fall you'll want to lean towards the colors which are apparent in your changing surroundings – hues of orange, yellow, and rust are examples of colors which lend themselves perfectly to the fall bouquet. Moreover, natural items such as berries, vines, plumed grasses, fall foliage, crab apple, high bush, or rose hips are fabulous accents which add a seasonal element to any arrangement.

Winter Weddings

When designing for winter weddings you will want to consider the colors and the materials that you see forming outside, even if poking put from beneath a bed of snow, such as forced bulbs, seedpods, holly, evergreens, and berries.

Seasonability and Price

Of course, an additional benefit to be had from choosing flowers which are in season is that they will typically yield the most impressive results for the most *reasonable prices*. Today, almost any flower can be found out of season, however, they are frequently not as healthy, and are usually significantly more costly, than those which are in season at the time.

Flowers that Turn You On

Perhaps the single most important rule when selecting flowers for the bouquets you design is to *choose those which turn you on*. To create a really exceptional bouquet, the individual flowers themselves will have to be exceptional. You should only be selecting flowers which *stir* you in some way emotionally, which create a reaction within you… flowers, whether fresh, silk, or dried which cause you to say, "*These* are gorgeous" the moment you lay your eyes on them. If you aren't getting that reaction, *keep looking*.

This is how exquisite designs and superior works are created.

Seasonal Availability

Earlier we provided a list of some of the most highly popular flowers for weddings, along with a short description of each. Following, listed according to their seasonal availability, colors, and their most common use, is a more extensive reference of flowers, greenery, fillers, and herbs which may be used for weddings. Although you are certainly not limited to these choices, you may find this reference helpful when planning your designs.

JANUARY

Item:	Colors:	Commonly Used:
Bells of Ireland	Green	Greenery/Flower
Bird of Paradise	Orange/Purple	Flower
Calla Lily (White)	White	Flower
Candytuft	White or Blush Pink	Filler
Daffodil	Yellow, White, Bi-colors	Flower
Delphinium	Blue, White, Purple	Flower
Eucalyptus	Bluish-Silvery Green	Greenery/ Filler
Heather	Pink	Filler
Leptospermum	Pink, White	Filler
Star Gazer Lily	Pink/White	Flower
Protea	Brown, Red, Yellow	Flower
Scabiosa	White, Blue, and Purple	Flower
Sweetpea	Pink, Purple, Red, White, Blue	Flower
Tulip	Red, Pink, White, Yellow Orange, Purple	Flower
Waxflower	White, Pink, Purple	Filler

FEBRUARY

Item:	Colors:	Commonly Used:
Bells of Ireland	Green	Greenery/Flower
Bird of Paradise	Orange/Purple	Flower
Calla Lily (White)	White	Flower
Candytuft	White or Blush Pink	Filler
Daffodil	Yellow, White, Bi-colors	Flower
Delphinium	Blue, White, Purple	Flower
Eucalyptus	Bluish-Silvery Green	Greenery/ Filler
Heather	Pink	Filler
Leptospermum	Pink, White	Filler
Lily (Star Gazer)	Pink/ White	Flower
Protea	Brown, Red, Yellow	Flower
Bells of Ireland	Green	Greenery/ Filler
Ranunculus	Yellow, Red, Pink, Purple, White, Cream	Flower
Scabiosa	White, Blue, and Purple	Flower
Sweetpea	Pink, Purple, Red, White, Blue	Flower
Tulip	Red, Pink, White, Yellow, Orange, Purple	Flower
Waxflower	White, Pink, Purple	Filler

MARCH

Flowers:	Colors:	Commonly Used:
Bells of Ireland	Green	Greenery/Flower
Bird of Paradise	Orange/Purple	Flower
Calla Lily (White)	White	Flower
Candytuft	White or Blush Pink	Filler
Daffodil	Yellow, White, Bi-colors	Flower
Delphinium	Blue, White, Purple	Flower
Eucalyptus	Bluish-Silvery Green	Greenery/ Filler
Godetia	Orange, Salmon, Pink Pink Bi-Color	Flower
Heather	Pink	Filler
Leptospermum	Pink, White	Filler
Lily (Star Gazer)	Pink/ White	Flower
Protea	Brown, Red, Yellow	Flower
Bells of Ireland	Green	Greenery/ Filler
Ranunculus	Yellow, Red, Pink, Purple, White, Cream	Flower
Scabiosa	White, Blue, and Purple	Flower
Sweetpea	Pink, Purple, Red, White, Blue	Flower
Tulip	Red, Pink, White, Yellow, Orange, Purple	Flower
Waxflower	White, Pink, Purple	Filler

APRIL

Item:	Colors:	Commonly Used:
Bells of Ireland	Green	Greenery/Flower
Bird of Paradise	Orange/Purple	Flower
Boronia	Pink	Filler
Calla Lily (White)	White	Flower
Candytuft	White or Blush Pink	Filler
Daffodil	Yellow, White, Bi-colors	Flower
Delphinium	Blue, White, Purple	Flower
Eucalyptus	Bluish-Silvery Green	Greenery/ Filler
Godetia	Orange, Salmon, Pink Pink Bi-Color	Flower
Heather	Pink	Filler
Leptospermum	Pink, White	Filler
Lily (Star Gazer)	Pink/ White	Flower
Lilies (Assorted)	White, Pink, Yellow, Orange, Red	Flower
Lisianthus	Pink, Purple, Yellow, Bi-colors	Flower, Filler
Peony	White, Pink, Red, Yellow	Flower
Protea	Brown, Red, Yellow	Flower
Ranunculus	Yellow, Red, Pink, Purple, White, Cream	Flower
Scabiosa	White, Blue, Purple	Flower
Sunflower	Yellow, Orange	Flower
Sweetpea	Pink, Purple, Red, White, Blue	Flower
Tulip	Red, Pink, White, Yellow, Orange, Purple	Flower
Veronica	Purple	Filler
Waxflower	White, Pink, Purple	Filler

MAY

Item:	Colors:	Commonly Used:
Asters	Pink, Purple, White	Flower
Bells of Ireland	Green	Greenery/Flower
Bird of Paradise	Orange/Purple	Flower
Calla Lily (White)	White	Flower
Candytuft	White or Blush Pink	Filler
Delphinium	Blue, White, Purple	Flower
English Lavender	Purple	Filler
Gladiola	White, Pink, Purple, Red, Yellow, Orange, Green	Flower
Godetia	Orange, Salmon, Pink Pink Bi-Color	Flower
Hydrangea	Pink, Blue, Purple, Green	Flower, Filler
Lily (Star Gazer)	Pink/ White	Flower
Lilies (Assorted)	White, Pink, Yellow, Orange, Red	Flower
Lisianthus	Pink, Purple, Yellow, Bi-colors	Flower, Filler
Love In A Mist	Pink, Yellow, Purple	Filler
Monte Casino	White, Purple	Filler
Peony	White, Pink, Red, Yellow	Flower
Protea	Brown, Red, Yellow	Flower
Ranunculus	Yellow, Red, Pink, Purple, White, Cream	Flower
Scabiosa	White, Blue, Purple	Flower
Statice	Purple, Pink, Blue, Cream Yellow	Filler
Sunflower	Yellow, Orange	Flower
Sweetpea	Pink, Purple, Red, White, Blue	Flower
Trachelium	Purple, Pink	Filler
Veronica	Purple	Filler
Waxflower	White, Pink, Purple	Filler
Yarrow	Yellow, Orange, Pink, White	Filler

JUNE

Item:	Colors:	Commonly Used:
Asters	Pink, Purple, White	Flower
Bells of Ireland	Green	Greenery/Flower
Calla Lily (White)	White	Flower
Candytuft	White or Blush Pink	Filler
Delphinium	Blue, White, Purple	Flower
English Lavender	Purple	Filler
Gladiola	White, Pink, Purple, Red, Yellow, Orange, Green	Flower
Godetia	Orange, Salmon, Pink	Flower
Hydrangea	Pink, Blue, Purple, Green	Flower, Filler
Lily (Star Gazer)	Pink/ White	Flower
Lilies (Assorted)	White, Pink, Yellow, Orange, Red	Flower
Lisianthus	Pink, Purple, Yellow, Bi-colors	Flower, Filler
Love In A Mist	Pink, Yellow, Purple	Filler
Monte Casino	White, Purple	Filler
Peony	White, Pink, Red, Yellow	Flower
Protea	Brown, Red, Yellow	Flower
Ranunculus	Yellow, Red, Pink, Purple, White, Cream	Flower
Scabiosa	White, Blue, Purple	Flower
Statice	Purple, Pink, Blue, Cream Yellow	Filler
Sunflower	Yellow, Orange	Flower
Sweetpea	Pink, Purple, Red, White, Blue	Flower
Trachelium	Purple, Pink	Filler
Tuberose	White, Blush Pink	Flower, Filler
Veronica	Purple	Filler
Yarrow	Yellow, Orange, Pink, White	Filler

JULY

Item:	Colors:	Commonly Used:
Asters	Pink, Purple, White	Flower
Bells of Ireland	Green	Greenery/Flower
Calla Lily (White)	White	Flower
Candytuft	White or Blush Pink	Filler
Delphinium	Blue, White, Purple	Flower
English Lavender	Purple	Filler
Gladiola	White, Pink, Purple, Red, Yellow, Orange, Green	Flower
Godetia	Orange, Salmon, Pink	Flower
Hydrangea	Pink, Blue, Purple, Green	Flower, Filler
Lily (Star Gazer)	Pink/ White	Flower
Lilies (Assorted)	White, Pink, Yellow, Orange, Red	Flower
Lisianthus	Pink, Purple, Yellow, Bi-colors	Flower, Filler
Love In A Mist	Pink, Yellow, Purple	Filler
Monte Casino	White, Purple	Filler
Phlox	Pink, Red, White, Purple	Filler
Protea	Brown, Red, Yellow	Flower
Ranunculus	Yellow, Red, Pink, Purple, White, Cream	Flower
Scabiosa	White, Blue, Purple	Flower
Statice	Purple, Pink, Blue, Cream Yellow	Filler
Sunflower	Yellow, Orange	Flower
Sweetpea	Pink, Purple, Red, White, Blue	Flower
Trachelium	Purple, Pink	Filler
Tuberose	White, Blush Pink	Flower, Filler
Veronica	Purple	Filler
Yarrow	Yellow, Orange, Pink, White	Filler

AUGUST

Item:	Colors:	Commonly Used:
Asters	Pink, Purple, White	Flower
Bells of Ireland	Green	Greenery/Flower
Calla Lily (Mini)	White, Yellow, Pink, Green, Orange, Red, Purple	Flower
Candytuft	White or Blush Pink	Filler
Delphinium	Blue, White, Purple	Flower
English Lavender	Purple	Filler
Gladiola	White, Pink, Purple, Red, Yellow, Orange, Green	Flower
Godetia	Orange, Salmon, Pink	Flower
Heather	Pink	Filler
Hydrangea	Pink, Blue, Purple, Green	Flower, Filler
Lily (Star Gazer)	Pink/ White	Flower
Lilies (Assorted)	White, Pink, Yellow, Orange, Red	Flower
Lisianthus	Pink, Purple, Yellow, Bi-colors	Flower, Filler
Love In A Mist	Pink, Yellow, Purple	Filler
Monte Casino	White, Purple	Filler
Phlox	Pink, Red, White, Purple	Filler
Protea	Brown, Red, Yellow	Flower
Scabiosa	White, Blue, Purple	Flower
Statice	Purple, Pink, Blue, Cream Yellow	Filler
Sunflower	Yellow, Orange	Flower
Sweetpea	Pink, Purple, Red, White, Blue	Flower
Trachelium	Purple, Pink	Filler
Tuberose	White, Blush Pink	Flower, Filler
Veronica	Purple	Filler
Yarrow	Yellow, Orange, Pink, White	Filler

SEPTEMBER

Item:	Colors:	Commonly Used:
Asters	Pink, Purple, White	Flower
Bells of Ireland	Green	Greenery/Flower
Calla Lily (Mini)	White, Yellow, Pink, Green, Orange, Red, Purple	Flower
Chinese Lanterns	Orange	Filler
Delphinium	Blue, White, Purple	Flower
English Lavender	Purple	Filler
Gladiola	White, Pink, Purple, Red, Yellow, Orange, Green	Flower
Godetia	Orange, Salmon, Pink	Flower
Heather	Pink	Filler
Hydrangea	Pink, Blue, Purple, Green	Flower, Filler
Leptospermum	Pink, White	Filler
Lily (Star Gazer)	Pink/ White	Flower
Lilies (Assorted)	White, Pink, Yellow, Orange, Red	Flower
Lisianthus	Pink, Purple, Yellow, Bi-colors	Flower, Filler
Love In A Mist	Pink, Yellow, Purple	Filler
Monte Casino	White, Purple	Filler
Ornamental Peppers	Orange, White, Red, Yellow	Filler
Phlox	Pink, Red, White, Purple	Filler
Protea	Brown, Red, Yellow	Flower
Scabiosa	White, Blue, Purple	Flower
Statice	Purple, Pink, Blue, Cream Yellow	Filler
Sunflower	Yellow, Orange	Flower
Trachelium	Purple, Pink	Filler
Tuberose	White, Blush Pink	Flower, Filler
Veronica	Purple	Filler
Yarrow	Yellow, Orange, Pink, White	Filler

OCTOBER

Item:	Colors:	Commonly Used:
Asters	Pink, Purple, White	Flower
Bells of Ireland	Green	Greenery/Flower
Calla Lily (Mini)	White, Yellow, Pink, Green, Orange, Red, Purple	Flower
Chinese Lanterns	Orange	Filler
Delphinium	Blue, White, Purple	Flower
English Lavender	Purple	Filler
Eucalyptus	Bluish-Silvery Green	Greenery/ Filler
Gladiola	White, Pink, Purple, Red, Yellow, Orange, Green	Flower
Godetia	Orange, Salmon, Pink	Flower
Heather	Pink	Filler
Hydrangea	Pink, Blue, Purple, Green	Flower, Filler
Leptospermum	Pink, White	Filler
Lily (Star Gazer)	Pink/ White	Flower
Lilies (Assorted)	White, Pink, Yellow, Orange, Red	Flower
Lisianthus	Pink, Purple, Yellow, Bi-colors	Flower, Filler
Love In A Mist	Pink, Yellow, Purple	Filler
Monte Casino	White, Purple	Filler
Ornamental Peppers	Orange, White, Red, Yellow	Filler
Phlox	Pink, Red, White, Purple	Filler
Protea	Brown, Red, Yellow	Flower
Scabiosa	White, Blue, Purple	Flower
Statice	Purple, Pink, Blue, Cream Yellow	Filler
Sunflower	Yellow, Orange	Flower
Trachelium	Purple, Pink	Filler
Tuberose	White, Blush Pink	Flower, Filler
Veronica	Purple	Filler
Yarrow	Yellow, Orange, Pink, White	Filler

NOVEMBER

Item:	Colors:	Commonly Used:
Asters	Pink, Purple, White	Flower
Bird of Paradise	Orange/Purple	Flower
Candytuft	White or Blush Pink	Filler
Delphinium	Blue, White, Purple	Flower
Eucalyptus	Bluish-Silvery Green	Greenery/ Filler
Gladiola	White, Pink, Purple, Red, Yellow, Orange, Green	Flower
Godetia	Orange, Salmon, Pink Pink Bi-Color	Flower
Heather	Pink	Filler
Leptospermum	Pink, White	Filler
Lilies (Assorted)	White, Pink, Yellow, Orange, Red	Flower
Lisianthus	Pink, Purple, Yellow, Bi-colors	Flower, Filler
Love In A Mist	Pink, Yellow, Purple	Filler
Monte Casino	White, Purple	Filler
Ornamental Peppers	Orange, White, Red, Yellow	Filler
Phlox	Pink, Red, White, Purple	Filler
Protea	Brown, Red, Yellow	Flower
Scabiosa	White, Blue, Purple	Flower
Statice	Purple, Pink, Blue, Cream Yellow	Filler
Sunflower	Yellow, Orange	Flower
Trachelium	Purple, Pink	Filler
Tuberose	White, Blush Pink	Flower, Filler
Veronica	Purple	Filler
Yarrow	Yellow, Orange, Pink, White	Filler

DECEMBER

Item:	Colors:	Commonly Used:
Bird of Paradise	Orange/Purple	Flower
Calla Lily (White)	White	Flower
Daffodil	Yellow, White, Bi-colors	Flower
Delphinium	Blue, White, Purple	Flower
Eucalyptus	Bluish-Silvery Green	Greenery/ Filler
Heather	Pink	Filler
Leptospermum	Pink, White	Filler
Lilies (Assorted)	White, Pink, Yellow, Orange, Red	Flower
Lisianthus	Pink, Purple, Yellow, Bi-colors	Flower, Filler
Protea	Brown, Red, Yellow	Flower
Scabiosa	White, Blue, Purple	Flower
Sweetpea	Pink, Purple, Red, White, Blue	Flower
Tulip	Red, Pink, White, Yellow, Orange, Purple	Flower
Waxflower	White, Pink, Purple	Filler

Seasonless Flowers & Herbs

The following flowers are commonly readily available all year in most markets, even though they may not be grown locally.

Flowers:

Orchids
Roses
Lilly of the Valley
Gardenia
Ivies
Most Greenery
Freesia
Stephanotis
Anemone
Forced Bulbs
Baby's Breath

Herbs:

Cat Mint
Salvia
Basil
Oregano
Marjoram
Sage - Purple, Tri-Color
Mint - Apple, Spear, Pepper, Orange, Chocolate
Lavender - Spanish, French, English
Rosemary
Lambs Ears
French Tarragon
Scented Geranium Foliage - Rose, Chocolate, Pepper, Staghorn

Floriography

Part of being a wedding floral design specialist includes having a wide base of knowledge about not only the techniques of floral design, but of the background, meaning, appropriateness and suitability of different types of flowers for the wedding or bride in question. In this section you'll acquire that base of specialized knowledge.

In assisting the bride with selecting her wedding blooms, you may want to recommend some flowers for the meaning attached to them, in order to incorporate special messages or significance into the arrangements and designs. In this way, you can help to create flowers for your client which are meaningful to her, not merely beautiful to look at.

The Language & Meaning of Flowers

From the beginning of time, flowers have held symbolic meanings which have been used in the communication of feelings and as means of expression.

Many of the romantic associations and meanings we attach to flowers today have their roots in the Victorian era. During the reign of Queen Victoria, the process of courtship became extremely complicated. It was not permissible for men and women to openly express their feelings for one another.

As a result, a system of secret codes soon developed by which men and women could express themselves to each other romantically.

This fascinating method of communication allowed women and men to express their feelings without violating the strict rules of social etiquette which dominated human interaction during this era.

A hint of desire could be communicated by the flutter of a fan. Calling cards often carried deeper meanings than what might appear on the surface. And flowers, especially, came to hold important meanings that were commonly used to express one's self.

For example, red roses could be used by a lady to express ardor, while yellow roses represented her jealously, and through a pink blossom she could communicate her refusal of a male suitor.

Gentlemen, likewise, could express their admiration of a lady through the use of flowers. Lilies expressed admiration for her purity, white roses for her innocence.

Flowers were used as subtle communication in every area of romance. They were used to announce love, they were used to refuse it - and they were used to express the wide range of feelings that existed between the two extremes.

These codes and symbolic meanings of flowers soon evolved into an elaborate 'language', which became officially termed as *floriography.*

The very first flower 'dictionary' or book of floriography was published in France during the Victorian era, in 1818. Entitled *Le Language des Fleurs* by Madame Charlotte de la Tour, the publication was almost instantly a sensation around the world.

Communicating Meaning Through Wedding Flowers: Tips & Ideas

Traditional or Historical Significance

You may suggest to the bride that you create a bouquet for her with a special meaning or message, or flowers which have a historical significance.

For example, for the bride to whom it is important to be historically traditional, you may suggest an armload of calla lilies – a highly traditional flower for weddings throughout history. Other traditional flowers that have remained popular over the centuries are orchids, hyacinths, gardenias, orange blossoms, stephanotis, and lily of the valley.

Sentimental Significance

Alternatively, suggest to the bride that you design her bouquet to incorporate sentimental significance. As an example, a bouquet of yellow tulips, may be just the thing for the bride who received that particular flower from her beloved on their very first date. Or perhaps the bride may wish to carry a small posy of lily of the valley because it is what her mother carried down the aisle on her wedding day. Another option for the bride, one which is rather whimsical and sentimental, is to spell out her fiance's name using flowers. For example, if her fiance's name is Rob, she might choose:

R – roses
O - orange blossoms
B - baby's breath

Individualized Bridesmaids Bouquets With Special Meaning

Suggest that the bride show her bridesmaids how much they mean to her through the design of personalized bridesmaid bouquets. Offer to individualize their bouquets by creating a slightly different bouquet for each girl which incorporates a special meaning, through the language of flowers, just for her. Don't forget to add a note with each bouquet which explains the meaning of each flower within it.

Selecting Flowers According to Meanings

Last, but by no means least, many brides today still favor the notion of selecting flowers for their bouquets based on the meanings those flowers have associated with them, just as the Victorians did.

The more sentiment you can incorporate into the bridal bouquet, the more romantic and meaningful it will be to the bride. When guiding the bride in making her selections, however, most importantly, she should choose those flowers which in some way move her spirit for reasons that may be impossible to even express.

Directory of The Meanings of Flowers

Flowers have a language all of their own, with different flowers all representing different symbolic meanings:

Amaryllis -- splendid beauty; *also* pride
Anemone -- expectation
Apple Blossoms -- good fortune, hope; *also* temptation
Baby's Breath -- pure heart; *also* innocence
Bachelor's Button -- Celibacy; *also* hope
Bellflower -- gratitude
Bluebells -- constancy
Blue Periwinkle -- friendship
Blue Violet -- faithfulness; *also* modesty
Buttercup -- riches
Calla Lily --magnificent beauty
Camellia -- perfect loveliness; *also* gratitude
Carnation -- distinction; *also* boldness (pink), love (red), talent (white); *also* pure, deep love
Cherry Blossom – chivalry
Christmas Rose – unselfish love
Chrysanthemum -- friendship; *also* truth; *also* prosperity
Crocus -- authority
Daffodil -- regard; *also* joy
Dahlia - gratitude
Daisy -- loyalty; *also* innocence; *also* share your feelings
Delphinium – well being
Fern - serenity
Flowering Almond -- constancy
Forget- Me-Not -- true love; *also* remembrance
Forsythia -- anticipation
Freesia -- innocence
Gardenia -- joy; *also* purity
Gerbera Daisy -- beauty
Gladiola – generosity; abundance; beauty
Iris – vitality
Hibiscus - glory
Holly -- foresight
Honeysuckle -- genuine affection; devoted affection; generous affection

Iris -- wisdom; *also* faith
Ivy -- fidelity
Jasmine -- amiability; *also* grace, elegance
Jonquil -- affection returned
Larkspur -- laughter
Lilac -- first love
Lily -- purity and innocence; *also* majesty; *also* truth; *also* honor
Lily of the Valley -- happiness
Lime blossoms -- conjugal bliss
Magnolia -- nobility; *also* appreciation of nature
Marigold -- affection; sacred affection
Mimosa -- secret love
Morning Glory -- affection
Myrtle -- love; love and remembrance
Orange Blossom -- purity; *also* fertility; *also* loveliness
Orchid -- beauty; rare beauty; *also* love
Pansy – thankfulness; friendship
Peony -- happiness; *also* bashfulness
Pine – vigorous life
Plum Blossom -- virtue
Poinsettia – Christmas joy
Red Chrysanthemum -- I love you; love
Red Rose -- passion; *also* "I love you"
Red Tulip -- love declared; declaration of love
Rose -- love; *also* deep love
Rosemary – remembrance

Stephanotis -- happiness in marriage
Sunflower -- adoration
Sweetpea -- delicate pleasures
Tulip -- love; *also* passion
Violet -- modesty; *also* faithfulness
Water Lily – companionship
White Camellia -- perfect loveliness
White Daisy -- innocence
White lilac -- first emotions of love
White Lily -- purity and innocence
White Rose - worthiness; *also* "I am worthy of you"
Wood Sorrel -- maternal love; *also* joy
Yellow Tulip -- hopeless love
Zinnia -- goodness

Meanings of Herbs:

Bay Laurel -- glory
Parsley -- beginnings
Rosemary -- love and remembrance
Sage -- immortality
Thyme -- courage, activity

Flower & Foliage Classifications In Design

In floral design, flowers and foliage are classified according to the type of role they will play in the design. These different categories help us to create specific types of visual effects in our arrangements. To create designs which have the best possible visual appeal and impact, you need to keep these flower classifications in mind as you are designing.

Flower Classifications In Design

There are three classifications of flowers: line flowers, filler flowers, and form flowers – all of which we will discussed directly below. As mentioned, there are similarly three classifications for foliage: line foliage, filler foliage, and form foliage – all of which we will describe under the next heading. When we are referring to the classification of flowers and foliage together, we call it line material, filler material, and form material.

Line Flowers

The line flowers in an arrangement define its horizontal and vertical dimensions. In other words line flowers give the arrangement height and breadth. Line flowers carry your eye away from the center of the design and towards the outer boundaries of the design.

Examples of flowers commonly used as line flowers are gladiola, snapdragons, delphinium, bells of Ireland, stock, band bird of paradise with stem included, the branches of blossoming tress such as cherry blossoms, and sometimes dried material such as sheathes of wheat for example.

Form Flowers (Secondary or Focal Flowers)

Also referred to as secondary or focal flowers, form flowers do the opposite of line flowers – the job of form flowers is to pull your eye *in towards the center* of the design, making you focus on the arrangement itself. In the average arrangement, form flowers will appear throughout the arrangement and will be used in enough abundance to make up the bulk of the arrangement.

Flowers commonly used for form are carnations, daisies, and chrysanthemums.

Filler Flowers

Filler flowers (occasionally referred to as *fill flowers*) are used to put the finishing touch on an arrangement and give it that final look of 'completeness'. We use filler flowers to fill in gaps or spaces which distract the eye by looking 'empty' in an arrangement. Filler flowers give a design a look of fullness and they make a design appear smooth, instead of allowing it to have a broken up appearance. This maintains harmony in the arrangement.

Most commonly, filler flowers are small, cluster-type flowers such as Babies Breath, English Statice, Queen Anne's Lace, or Lily of the Valley.

Foliage Classifications In Design

In floral design, foliage is also classified according to the type of role it will play in the design. There are two classifications of foliage: line foliage and secondary foliage. You will notice that some types of foliage can be used as both line foliage as well as form foliage, depending on the manner in which they are used and displayed. For example, a branch of ivy can be used as line foliage if left very long, but can also serve very well as form foliage when it is clipped into short sprigs.

Line Foliage

The concept behind line foliage is identical to that of line flowers. The line foliage in an arrangement defines the arrangement's horizontal and vertical dimensions, giving it height and breadth. Line foliage carries your eye away from the center of the design and towards the outer boundaries of the design. Foliage used for line foliage needs to have fairly straight-line structures.

Examples of foliage commonly used for line foliage would be cedar, eucalyptus, ivy, and fern.

Form Foliage

Also referred to as secondary foliage, form foliage does the opposite of line foliage by drawing your eye in to the center of the design, making you focus on the arrangement itself. In the average arrangement, form foliage will appear throughout the arrangement in bulk and will therefore be a dominant element in the design. Foliage used for form foliage needs to be able to give the impression of fullness, as opposed to length.

Examples of foliage commonly used for form or secondary foliage would be ivy, fern, boxwood, and holly.

[This page intentionally left blank]

Unit Summary and Review

Congratulations! You've completed your first unit of the course and are now one step closer to becoming a highly skilled wedding floral designer. Are you feeling excited? Ready to keep going?

Keep up the good work! Move on to Unit 2 and then the other units in the course, and before long you'll have the ability to earn your living working with brides every day, designing beautiful flower arrangements for real weddings.

You've learned a lot in this introductory unit and you now have a solid foundation of knowledge for the design principles, techniques and methods that you will be learning in future units.

In Unit One we took you all the way back to 3000 B.C. and gave you a look at what the earliest wedding flowers were like, then we continued on that journey through history to the present day. You'll be able to draw upon this knowledge to incorporate history and tradition into your designs when you start designing for clients and their weddings.

We talked about the importance and role of flowers in a wedding, as well as the importance of your role as the wedding floral designer.

We looked at a breakdown of weddings by month to give you an idea of when the weddings are taking place; this will help you to know what to expect from a time management perspective throughout the year and will help you prepare for your busier or peak seasons as a wedding floral designer.

We also discussed the most popular types of flowers that are used in wedding floral design and took a fascinating look into floriography and the language and meaning of flowers. This will allow you to design arrangements for your brides that are truly personalized and meaningful for them - which is precisely what every bride craves. We provided you with an easy to use reference guide that you can consult again and again when you are looking to inject the right symbolism and meaning into the arrangements you design for your clients well into the future, and long after you have completed this course. In addition, we looked at other factors that should be taken into consideration when you are designing flowers for a wedding in order to really match the flowers to the couple and to the specific wedding in a meaningful and personal way.

And finally, we took a look at the three basic classifications of flowers and foliage and how they are applied in floral design.

It's this type of advanced knowledge that your clients will appreciate and will recognize in you as being the mark of an expert and professional.

[This page intentionally left blank]

Coming Up in the Program ...

We're just getting warmed up! You've completed the first unit of the course - which was an introductory look at wedding floral design. If you wish to continue on with the full course and earn your certification as a Wedding Floral Designer, there are eleven more units to study. In the next unit you'll move into design theory where we'll explore the foundation upon which all good design is built - topics like the elements and principles of design, and color theory. This is the stuff every good designer learns, in every field of design, because it gives you the building blocks to create truly amazing designs once you start learning the hands-on methods and techniques a little later on.

After completing the next unit, as you move further on through the course, in subsequent units we'll get into the all the step by step techniques and methods for designing the various different styles of bouquets, corsages, boutonnieres, flower girl arrangements, church flower arrangements, and reception flowers including centerpiece design and spatial arrangements... and more. In later lessons, we'll also get down to the finishing details and teach you the professional tricks for turning ordinary arrangements into *extraordinary* ones (such as pretty stem wrap methods for bouquets as just one example).

As you move through the course you'll be working hands-on, and you'll have the fun of designing as you learn.

Are you excited to move on to Unit Two? Let's do it! If you haven't yet got your Unit Two lesson material, you should register for the course now to keep your focus and momentum going. For maximum benefit, you should always try to move from one lesson unit to the next with as little interruption as possible so that your learning experience is cohesive and you stay motivated! Every lesson is designed to build upon the one before it, so go through the course exactly as it was intended and designed, one lesson right after the other! Soon you'll be designing stunning floral arrangements for weddings and you'll will have the pride and satisfaction of putting this new skill set into use.

Here's What You'll Learn in the Next Unit

DESIGN THEORY

The Elements of Design

Form

Line

Texture

Size

Space

Shape

Pattern

The Principals of Design

Balance

Contrast

Movement

Rhythm

Proportion

Scale

Dominance

Unity

Harmony

Color

Color in Wedding Floral Design

The Role of Color

Color Symbolism

Factors in Selecting Color

Color and Reception Flowers

Color Theory

What's Next?

How to Proceed on to Unit Two and the Rest of the Course

Congratulations! You've completed Unit 1 of the course!

Unit 1 was a light introduction into the world of wedding floral design, to help you get you into the headspace of thinking like a wedding floral designer. We don't want to overwhelm you by diving too deep too quickly, so Unit 1 was designed just to help you get your feet wet. As you proceed on to the other remaining eleven units of the course, the lessons become more and more in-depth, yet always easy to understand, fun and exciting.

Enroll in the full program to continue on to the remaining eleven units, and you'll soon be well on your way to earning your certificate in Wedding Floral Design from The International Institute of Weddings.

Go From Beginner to Advanced in Just a Few Months

You'll learn *absolutely everything* you need to design beautiful wedding flowers, using all of the proper, professional techniques. Learn the Elements and Principles of Design, Color Theory, Styles of Design, How to Design With Fresh Flowers, Processing and Conditioning Fresh Flowers, How to Wire Stems, How to Design With Silk Flowers, The Different Styles and Types of Bouquets, How to Design Bouquets, How to Wire Bouquets, How to Design With Bouquet Holders, How to Create Stem Wraps, How to Design Bouquets With Special Features, The Different Types and Styles of Corsages, How to Design Corsages, The Different Types and Styles of Boutonnieres, How to Design Boutonnieres, How to Design Flower Girl Arrangements, The Different Types and Styles of Reception Flowers, How to Design Reception Arrangements, The Different Types and Styles of Ceremony Arrangements, How to Design Ceremony Arrangements, Proper Protocols for Setting Up Flower Arrangements in Churches and Reception Venues, and still much more. Step by step, fully illustrated design instructions, techniques, and methods are included. *Go from beginner to advanced in just a few months.*

Are you excited to keep going?

See the next page for an irresistible offer you won't want to pass up - you'll get to enroll in the rest of the program *entirely risk free*, backed by our 30 Day Money Back Guarantee - and you can cancel at any time if you aren't 100% satisfied.

[This page intentionally left blank]

Enroll in the Rest of the Course Now, Risk Free

30 Day Money Back Guarantee.

Cancel at Anytime If You are Not 100% Satisfied

If the thought of becoming a fully trained and certified Wedding Floral Designer excites you, enroll in the full program now. You have nothing to lose. We make it easy for you to try the course, entirely risk free. Enroll now and you can cancel anytime within 30 days for a full refund if you are not completely satisfied.

After you enroll, you will receive a new unit of course material each month for the next eleven months. We're confident you'll be delighted with the program, just like the hundreds of other highly satisfied students who have gone through the program over the last ten years. But if for any reason you are not satisfied, you can cancel at anytime.

Upon successful completion of the full program and all course units, you will earn your certificate from The Institute of Weddings and the prestigious credential of *Certified Wedding Floral Designer.*

Enroll Today With Complete Confidence
Thanks to a 30-Day Money-Back Guarantee

How to Enroll

To enroll now, completely risk free, simply go to the following page at the Institute of Weddings:

www.instituteofweddings.com/enroll-now

If you have difficulty finding that page, simply use the contact form on the web site to request assistance, and a friendly Institute of Weddings representative will be pleased to help you.

[This page intentionally left blank]

Sign Up for Our
Floral Design Newsletter

Receive Free Floral Design Tips & Ideas, Tricks of the Trade, the Latest Design Trends, Insiders Secrets for Selling Your Floral Design Services, Special Floral Design Related Offers and Savings - and more.

We will never provide your email address to any outside third party and we won't flood your email box - we just send the occasional message with genuinely useful information. And you can unsubscribe any time.

Subscribe for Free Here:

www.InstituteOfWeddings.com/subscribe

[This page intentionally left blank]

About the Course

The Wedding Floral Design Course by the International Institute of Weddings™ is a highly specialized training program focusing *exclusively* on wedding floral design. No funeral flowers or hospital arrangements like the lessons in so many other floral design courses – instead, we'll focus intensively on designing *flowers for weddings* – and *only* weddings. After all, weddings are where the glamour and excitement is!

If your passion is *weddings*, funeral flowers simply won't inspire you, so we've designed a program with laser sharp focus, for people just like you. And if you're thinking of turning your floral design skills into a business, career, or even some extra income in your spare time, **weddings are DEFINITELY where the money is.**

"I tried to find wedding floral design classes in my local area and all the classes were so expensive, most didn't even focus on wedding flowers which is really where my interest is, plus I didn't like the scheduling for those local wedding floral design classes. Learning from home has been great. In the end I'm really glad I took this home study wedding floral design course instead of those less specialized floral design classes in my community. This course is much more thorough - I would have had to take numerous classes at much greater expense to learn what I've learned through this wedding floral design course. Thank you again. "

– Anabella Martinez, Dallas, Texas

Satisfied Students Around the World - Since 1999

Every year hundreds of highly satisfied students use Institute of Weddings™ training programs to successfully pursue their dreams within the wedding industry. Since 1999 students have told us that our distance education training programs have changed their lives, opened up new doors of opportunity for them, and made it possible for them to live their dreams. Weddings are such an exciting field and we take great pride and satisfaction in giving our students the specialized knowledge and skills they need to enjoy a future doing something they love in this exciting industry. We want to help you do the same; we are committed to your success, and to providing you with a rewarding and enjoyable learning experience.

[This page intentionally left blank]

Also From *The International Institute of Weddings*™:

"How to Start and Operate a Wedding Floral Design Business"

Start Your Own Wedding Floral Design Business From Home. Turn your knack for floral design into a profitable business. Learn how to start and operate a profitable wedding floral design business from your own home. This in-depth self-study business training manual is for the individual who already has some basic floral design ability and wants to learn how to successfully turn it into their own business. It is intended to help you transform your existing talent for floral design -- even if you are self-taught or dabbling as a hobby -- into a profitable and viable home based business.

You'll learn everything from the correct pricing formulas used by wedding florists for achieving maximum profit, to proven marketing & promotional methods for attracting clients, as well as operating procedures for the home based wedding floral designer, complete with proven, highly successful business concepts you can model your own business after. You'll be guided step by step through finding clients and establishing yourself within your local market. You'll learn how to correctly set up your business, how to do a consultation with a client, how to create a contract. Sample forms and contracts are included for you to model your own. The course reveals the trade secrets that can otherwise take years of experience to acquire. Get the insider's edge to put your wedding floral business on the fast track.

"All I can say about the course is WOW!!!!!!! I skimmed through the whole thing as soon as I got it. Then I actually read through it. Now I'm working on actually studying it, taking notes, working out plans, etc. It is so well-written and so down-to-earth!! I appreciate that you touch on subjects that someone else might think would be assumed — like projecting an image, etc. The fact that I have you behind me on this adventure means so very very much to me!! THANKS!!! "

Jan Putzner, Michigan

We'll show you exactly how to pump more profit out of your business by incorporating rental items. We'll show you how to buy wholesale. We'll lead you through the proven formula to establish yourself as a major player within your local marketplace - yes even if you operate from home. And you will learn the hottest, most powerful ways of promoting and marketing your wedding floral design business - because if you don't have customers, you don't have a business.

All of this information is presented in a easy to follow, fully comprehensive training manual consisting of over 179 pages. Start your new business soon - full time or part time. Enjoy the pride and self-satisfaction of business ownership.
 If the thought of turning your knack for floral design into an income-generating business excites you, this self-study course is an excellent way to get started now and be in business soon with very low overhead and very low start-up expenses. We give you a complete proven and tested system. All instruction is given in an easy to follow, step-by-step format. Continually updated and revised, this in-depth, fully comprehensive self-study course has been the only one of its kind in the industry for over a decade and has successfully helped thousands of other individuals just like you to launch their own wedding floral businesses.

**Available at
www.InstituteOfWeddings.com/wedding-floral-business**

Or simply go to InstituteOfWeddings.com and find this course listed under Courses and Certification in the navigation bar.

Other Courses by The Institute of Weddings™

Start or Grow Your Wedding Business Today With Leading-Edge Wedding Career Courses and Training Programs by the Prestigious International Institute of Weddings™

All of the courses listed here can be found on InstituteOfWeddings.com, under the "Courses and Certification" heading, or you can directly type the url of the course you are interested in, listed below. If you have any difficulty finding the courses you are looking for, please feel free to contact the Institute of Weddings using the contact link on the website, and a representative will promptly assist you.

How to Start and Operate a Wedding Floral Design Business
www.InstituteOfWeddings.com/ wedding-floral-business

Certified Wedding Planner Course
www.weddingplannercourse.com

Certified Wedding Stylist Course
www.certifiedweddingstylist.com

Certified Theme Wedding Planner Course
www.instituteofweddings.com/ theme-wedding-planner-certification

More courses are added often. Visit the Institute of Weddings website for the current course offerings at InstituteOfWeddings.com.

About the International Institute of Weddings™

Since 1999, The International Institute of Weddings™ has been providing some of the most in-depth professional training and education available in the wedding industry anywhere world-wide. We set the standard for excellence in wedding-related training with our in-depth and extensive course curriculums, and exclusive certifications for wedding professionals. As one of the longest established training organizations within the wedding industry, The Institute of Weddings™ is one of the true innovators and leaders in the field of training within the wedding industry. Learn more about The Institute of Weddings™, or see all of the courses currently offered by visiting the Institute's website online at: www.InstituteOfWeddings.com

Contact The Institute of Weddings™

If there is anything we can assist you with, please feel free to contact us directly and we'll be happy to reply to you promptly and personally. Use the Contact Form you'll find at:

InstituteOfWeddings.com

[This page intentionally left blank]

Printed in the USA
CPSIA information can be obtained
at www.ICGtesting.com
LVHW071203280124
770159LV00013B/1848